FORWARD TWO

ISBN 979-8-9893320-1-4

Walnut Street Publishing
1645 S Holtzclaw Ave
Chattanooga, TN 37404

Forward Two

Poems

Kat McKay

WALNUT STREET
—PUBLISHING—

Poems

Peaches

In somebody else's poem about me,

there's probably something about peaches,
something about *mammal fuzz, sun-rosed skin,*
supple, yielding flesh.

A *tearing.*

Juicy sweetness,
parted from the stony, pitted center.

Maybe
a smell of imminent decay,
the peak of bruised ripeness.

Nothing about how I'm allergic,
like the lady in *Parasite*,
throat closed by a capful
of innocence.

Nothing about how I'm really more like
the jolt of Mountain Dew lemons
than anything Edenically derived.

Jolene

I watch you over 82 miles between our mouths I
watch you over three months cut short by a
20-minute phonecall I watch your mouth
on her mouth.

I watch my own disembodied wailing in the
pumproom I watch my lifeguards bang on the
door watch me trapped crushed I watch her on
your Snapchat, once I watch her in Greece 8200
miles between your mouths I watch her come
back to you I watch you shove me further
tearing my calcified just-a-break shell I watch
myself, drunk wailing on the newborn floor of
my dormroom, dial seven numbers, once I watch
you on my way to calc stoop to put your mouth
on her mouth I watch that replay inbetween diff
eqs not breathing

I'm off Insta, don't watch anyone for a while and
I don't text back

@queerappalachia

O sage, impart to me your wisdom.
I come freshly-washed from the Borders of
Hickdom, newly-matriculated from Redacted,
Tennessee, from the high school with the
least-muddy Jeeps, least Copenhagen-worn
pockets, whose students emphatically distance
themselves from their rednekkid cousins across
the river, wending FM dials up narrow tracks
between Luke Combs and Morgan Wallen.

I come with some questions, in search of your
guidance. What is my place in this world? How
can I fix it?

I come to you shaky and cold, weathered by the
ridgeline winds of my penultimate year in
Knoxville. I love how you have become who you
are, a Hydran chorus shrieking to be known and
understood. Take me under your collective
batwing, fold me into your warm possum-pouch.
Owl-swallow me whole, hork me out in shapely
pellets.

pre-med vs. a smaller howl
italics *from Gavin, from Michigan*

My parents said I come from the mountains,
birthed from caverns undercut by steady
dripping, in the air only *if I come* when you call.
In your sleep, remember me as someone known.
Forget me in each moment of sweat-stained
waking, *back home* shaking and screaming
through ancestral rhododendron tunnels. I
follow you, marked *with a southern*-pointed
tri-star, with my bat-crepe ears attuned to your
heartbeat-secret *accent*, track each powdered
swath through the wildness you talk down to.
But if they knew, *they'd* drown me in the Ocoee,
let me gurgle turgid TVA waters, keep company
with ghost boaters. Honey, *kill me.* Bury me in
red clay, wreathed in sprigs of mountain laurels.

Kat, *sometimes*, other times unfolding into fullmoon banshee, ridden stripped nekkid in Appalachian liminals. *I can't tell* whether I have always been what you think I am, whether I've calcified with each successive slur, *whether your accent's* syncopated terror or unneeded protection, gene-splicing for extinct hemlocks. Are you *real or* something dream-croaked from my gullet? Can you hear the upper howl of my ultraviolent primal rage? *put on* my molted iridescent cottonmouth skin, dismiss with your faded and practical lexicon, let me in and listen to me.

a recipe for the way my dad makes sweet tea

1. Grumble a little about how we don't have anything sweet in the house. Reach around behind you with closed fists and rub the small of your back with your knuckles. Open the cabinet that usually holds the Oreos. Close the cabinet that usually holds the Oreos.

2. Gaze, once again, into the cabinet that usually holds the Oreos. Holler into the living room: "Krista, we got any Oreos?" taking the resounding, suburban silence issuing from the living room as a negative answer.

2b. If it is between Easter and mid-September, continue to make tea, regardless of the presence or absence of Oreos.

3. As you mentally commit yourself to making tea, cease to grumble and begin to hum, softly, under your breath. This is a pleasurable event,

and you've already got some endorphins swirling around at the mere anticipation of the tea.[1][2]

4. Open the lower cabinet, where the glass pot sits. There will be a non-negligible amount of clattering pots. This cannot be helped, since Krista has banished the tea-making pot to the back of the cabinet. Do not even think of making the tea in another pot, since the glass pot is what your mom made tea in.[3]

---

[1] The relationship between Southerners and their tea, or at least my father and his tea, is simple. It feels absolutely incredible to sip something cold while mowing the lawn, jolted with just enough caffeine to still let you sleep at night, sinuses cleared from the rampant pollen, humidity, grass-fumes by the gentle kick of lemon, throat lubricated gently and mind imperceptibly soothed by the syrupy sweetness. And it's dirt cheap. There's something of Appalachian blue-collar Protestantism in the simple heavenliness of sweet tea. Paying a dollar for a Coke from McDonald's is unfathomable, for the double sinful excesses of un-frugality and sloth-inducing, diabetes-provoking amounts of high-fructose corn syrup and heaven knows what other chemicals.

[2] God, it's been so long since I've done a good footnote.

[3] This pot is of mysterious origins. Tempered, smoky brown glass, no lid, that you can put directly on the stovetop. No embossed brand name, no Made In ___ sticker.

5. Fill the pot with tap water. If you are in a hurry, which you usually are, crank the tap up to full heat. Stick your fingers into the deluge, wait for it to really burn before whipping the pot under the stream. This allegedly reduces the time it takes the water to boil.

6. Whirl the pot around to the stove, place it on the back burner. Fumble around with those gas knobs that you still haven't quite gotten the hang of, the ones you have to prime and click and otherwise fiddle with. Your fiddling produces what seems to be an excessive amount of gas-smell, almost fogging up the kitchen.

7. Think only a little of horrifically, accidentally gas-poisoning your family, suffocating in your well-insulated home. Alternatively, of a fireball sparked by the click of the neat blue eye-flame, engulfing the kitchen you've just had redone. Turn on the fan in the hood to full blast, a roaring, overpowered vacuum that drowns out

Krista's concerned inquiries shouted from the living room.

8. While the water is getting to boiling, prepare the receptacle of the tea. Pull the big plastic pitcher from the other cabinet. Not the glass one, since you'll be subjecting the tea to destructive, shattering changes in temperature. Besides, what is this, Thanksgiving?

9. Shake about an inch-thick layer of normal white granulated sugar into the bottom of the pitcher, straight from the yellow Domino's bag. Squirt in an equal amount of ReaLemon juice, from the green bottle in the door of the fridge. Eyeballing is fine, you'll adjust to taste later.

10. Go ahead and grab the big box of Family Size Lipton tea bags[4] from the top shelf of the cabinet, and submerge two or three packets into the pot, which should now be boiling.

11. Take you a slotted spoon and stir the lemon-sugar mixture wildly, until you hear the grittiness of the sugar rubbing against the sides of the pitcher change in timbre, indicating a slight dissolvement of its crystalline structure.

12. Turn off the stove and the hood fan, leaving the pot steaming where it is on the back burner. While you let the tea steep, mosey into the den, flip through TV channels for about 20 minutes

---

[4] Again, the relationship between Southerners and their tea is uncomplicated. We couldn't pick a tea plant out of a lineup, will never even visit a climate where it is possible to grow tea, much less meet a tea farmer. We don't host elaborate tea ceremonies or read anybody's futures in the soggy leaves. We sure as shit had nothing to do with that Tea Party business or any of those plantations over there in India or wherever. The brown powder in the packet exists only to go into the pot and steep. I think this is the same way that, to people in other places, watermelon comes in triangles, without seeds.

or until your suspicions that nothing good is on are confirmed. Sigh, and lever yourself off the couch and back into the kitchen.

13. Pour the tea into the pitcher.

14. Stir again with the slotted spoon, really scraping the bottom until the gritty rubbing of the sugar crystals stops.[5] Taste a little bit from the edge of the slotted spoon. Add more sugar or lemon juice to taste. Since you've been making sweet tea for decades, you shouldn't have to add anything, but it's nice just to check.

---

[5] Number one rookie mistake of making sweet tea is putting sugar into tea that is already cold. The heat of the tea is what dissolves the sugar, duh, forming a syrup that evenly permeates and sweetens the tea instead of leaving individual grains that sink to the bottom. However, if one did have a supply of already-cold unsweet tea, simple syrup or honey (or agave nectar for the millennial vegans) can be added more easily. But why the fuck anybody not suffering from the sugar-wary health-consciousness of advanced old age would choose to have unsweet tea just sitting around their fridge is beyond me.

15. Top off the pitcher with cold tap water. This is an integral step for several reasons. First, since you used an incredibly high ratio of tea/lemon/sugar to boiling water, the tea is now very concentrated, visibly thicker and more viscous than it has any right to be. Second, you are working with an incredibly complex thermodynamic process here. If you were to, for instance, put the tea straight into the fridge, or even add ice cubes directly into the still-hot tea, you would compromise the whole sapidity of the pitcher. Nobody likes tea flavored with the freezer burn of stale ice, and you can almost taste a tea that has been shunted into the fridge too quickly, like how still-hot leftovers will steam up their tupperwares and get all soggy. Finally, before you scoff at the pedestrian tappiness of the water, understand that the minerals in Bradley County tap water are some of the best in the world. We've got both a Crystal Geyser and a Deer Park plant right down the road. I must say, whatever blend of trace metals is in Bradley County tap water adds a subtle

richness, a fuller body to balance both the bitter acidity and sickly sweetness of the tea.

15. Now put the tea in the fridge.

16. Watch some TV while the tea cools. This process could take several hours, depending on the fulness of the fridge and whether anything good is on.

17. When the tea is cool, change into your lawn-mowing clothes-- white T-shirt, paint-spattered cargo shorts, the tennis shoes with the holes in the toes.

18. Pour the tea from the pitcher into your styrofoam cup, the one you've been saving and rinsing out for months now. No ice, shouldn't need it if it's been in the fridge for long enough, and it'll just melt soon as you step outside anyways.

19. Give it a little taste, just to where you feel refreshed enough to fathom the 95% humidity

out there.[6] Your body is already sweating in resigned anticipation.

20. Leave the cup of tea in the relatively cool shade on the top step of the back porch while you mow the lawn, returning periodically to sip/gulp prodigiously from it.

---

[6] It's not actually raining, the sun is very much offensively out, but each breath feels *wet,* like the air is a load of towels that didn't get dried all the way. If you draw your finger up your forearm, you can gather condensation from the beading hairs, flick it and watch it spatter on the concrete.

sweet tea
after Anthony

fresh-brewed
translucent carmel skin

shock of ice in the still-steamy glass:
goosebumps.

soft sugar-hills dissolve slowly,
imperfect residue
grates against tongue.

teeth clink together,
shaky-caffeine buzz,
quaking legs.

and just enough lemon
brightens Friday afternoon

as I guzzle
your southern nectar
into me

The papermill is grown over with weeds.

                    Where my papaw worked,
            twelve hours a day for seventeen years.
        Where with a hook the size of your arm he
                would take and drive the hook
        into a log that had come rolling off the truck
            take the log and drive the hook into it
                and take the log and sling it around
                    a corner of the chute and then
        sling his hook out of the log and turn back
around and take his hook and hook the next log
                and sling it around into the chute
            where the really unlucky folks worked
                and would take the log that Papaw
        had slung off his hook the size of your arm and
            take the log and grind it up into paper.

            Twelve hours a day, for seventeen years.

Three growing boys and a spittin'-mad woman at home, standing in the kitchen, wood-panelling shone with bacon grease, standing in front of the dark wood, the hewn logs, coughing.

The papermill is grown over with weeds.

The people who used to run the mill sell insurance now. After wearing through a workforce that could hook logs with a hook the size of your arm and take and sling them around into a chute and then turn around and hook the next log twelve hours a day for seventeen years, the people who told my papaw to hook the logs sell insurance to people with complicated and expensive sicknesses. People who smelled the wet pulp of rotten, steaming logs twelve hours a day for seventeen years. Who went home and drank themselves stupid to wash out the taste. Who stood in the kitchen and coughed.

The papermill is grown over with weeds.

There's a hole in the earth where
the chute used to be.
The log-hooks are rusted through,
spotted with lacey lichen.
Crumbled tires, bent frames.
Nests in the paper tanks.

He must have stood here, slung like this.

Papaw is grown over with weeds.
I think, I've never been.

Honeysuckle and kudzu. Ragweed and
deadnettle and blackberry brambles.
Yellow flowers and deep purple against green
and the little white ones that smell like jasmine.

Liminal Spaces

I. Market Square

You are shuttered restaurants, wrought iron
patio chairs stacked, twinkle lights unplugged.
You are expensive night sky napkins, already
tented on marble tabletops for god knows who.
You are ice melting in champagne buckets,
littered gold foil torn from goosenecks. You are
ghost-crowds in the bars, smuggled wine in your
Hydroflask, the warm bump of elbows. You are
the buzz of silence in my ears, the loudest sound
this week.

You are the bandstand, the space between two
unknowns, tai-chi your way between voids,
swing me onto darkened stage. Tapdance away
apocalypse. You are eye contact over Zoom,
headlights through fog.

You are the first fruit, blackberries.
Sour and pitted kisses, sweat-stained
and pale, candied in pink wine.

II. Tuesday?

You are the slow rising of bread
the bubbling of unshowered yeast.

You are roof asphalt scraping
on shorted thighs perched on the peak
of Fort Sanders, the stretching of time
like kneading dough, raccoons
growing bolder, wafting smoke
of butts and finished bottles
dropped down the chimney.

You are thin skin waiting for pink
thunderstorms, shivering into a lemony high,
doughy mud caked on fingers, surrounded
sneezing by dogwood and azaleas.

III. Untitled
    after Aslan

I said I wouldn't do anything ever again,
I'm not doing this again.

Every time you come, sweatshirted, I leave
lonelier, a wolf masked in a sheep that only calls
for all of my meaty discussion posts.

I still let you cover me in fecund salty
showers-are-for-grocery-days sweat,
teach me the science of epidemiology,
tend your tempered immune
system to brave this solo voyage.

Drench me in sweet sticky
unbrushedness of teeth,
rip down my throat into
my bedroom, porch, bedroom, porch,
turn me into your mask.

And yet, I always have to clean off me.
I've learned that even when I don't,
I still have a habit of spilling
out of my own mind and staining my protective
barriers.

Your bedroom, porch, bedroom, porch:
my spaces are no longer my own,
my body, cradle of disease, has been claimed.

Moon Garden

Leftovers secrete between my newel posts,
drip through bannister spindles.

Ceres herself hovers in my crawlspace
holding her shears ready
for cooped-up, cookie-cut me.

I plant myself in her flowerbeds,
an infinite backyard of violent absolutions.
Crocuses endlessly propagate from permafrost.

I don't have enough spangles for six hefty
sorrows.
A spasming constellation gasps for air.

The sky flagrates, wholly alight.
Bleeds offal, burns rotten waste.

Fountain City Lanes

He sees her emerge from the backroom, whiffs
hints of remembered sweat.

She sprays piles of returned shoes, sanitizes her
grimace, turns to him, reads the Tuesday night
special: two games and a pitcher, seven dollars.

It's 9:30, so she sighs, stoops under the counter,
flips on the blacklight, transforms tired disco
into something worse.

He wishes her cigarette breaks would align
with the spaces between his frames.

Panting, he scuffs, slides into each throw,
balances on rented heel-edge, left wing
outflung, right foot flagged back.

He turns over his shoulder to see if she saw,
clunking pins keep time to his heart.

He wishes he was ambidextrous enough to fit his
fingers inside her and keep his ball hand free.

He secretes grease onto lane thirty-four, drops
hints with each crack of plastic on hardwood,
spins out further and further.

He reaches 160 years into suburban history,
imagines his fervid ardor mapped on the only
myth he knows:

Some time ago, a small and lonely widower, lost
in aimless grief, digs a hole in the valley below
his wife's grave.

It broadens into an acre-and-a-half depression,
heart-shaped, for her to look down on from
heaven. He fills it with tears, installs a fountain.

The lake attracts aggressive geese, gives its
name to Knoxville scaffoldry: Fountain City.

But now the park flickers under orange lamps,
stolen cigarettes tossed in pairs on cracking
playgrounds.

The bowler wishes to bury his lover
in a heart-shaped hole, to fill it
with hosewater and breadcrumbs,

prays for waterfowl to change their
migration patterns, for just enough
courage to say something,

to quickstep up to the second dotted line,
hurl something heavy and holey straight at her.

to knock out her front teeth with
his warmth, tip his ball back out
of the gutter, strike something.

He loves her. He is going to throw up.
He is ready to let her into the ground.

The Pigeon River

She flies along I-40, down the world's oldest
river gorge, carves through Appalachia,
millimeter by millennia. Greasy raft guides
nickname her *Dirty Bird*, sustained through
summers on her poisoned meat, marinated in
layers of highway sludge. She infects them with
c. diff, trenchfoot, but she's warmer than the
Nantahala, less prone to church groups and
rockslides. On peak-season weekends,
raft-enameled tourists clog her eddies, pause for
ziplocced-phone photo ops.

Having ignored the desperate calls of their
undertipped guide, their raft folds, overtips on
Rooster Tail. They refuse to *swim to the boat*,
float serenely towards rapids beiging into
whitenoise.

Life-jacketed dogs skitter upcurrent, watch
their humans deboat for Marlboros sifted from
drybags, ash butts on limestone.

Left of Exit 447, above the Pigeon, deer twitches
atop startled minivan, drains to the river below.
A native Hartfordian pulls up behind the skittish
mother ignoring his murmured *y'all want that?*
mid-insurance call. He loads carcass into
beatered red pickup, plans deepfreezer tetris,
feasts to come.

Dry-suited kayakers return to the Pigeon in
mid-November, revel in her winter plumage
bereft of tourists, drop relentlessly into her
windpipe, clogged with meltwater.

To your left, you'll see the Appalachians,
oldest mountains in the world.

Phenomenal Spray
the Vol Wall, Knoxville

I worked at a climbing gym for two years
Before the world was changed, and then after.

The building was a bunker, cavernous
rec rooms carved under our campus across the
river from oak ridge, a maze of cinderblocks and
odd steam vents, untraceable chlorine, echoed
whistleblasts and dim racketball shots.

Our gym, the Wall, shared a floor with the judo
club, evenings. They pushed dustmops across
the foam mats, against the chalk dust, stretched
in unison and pawed tensely at eachother.

The climbers clap, send up small puffs of chalk
powder from the bags at their hips, from the
anthills on the mats. You can smell it in the air,
sharp mineral feet tang.

It hangs, dusting. Waits to be wiped away.

Scrawny mops of hair stare at angled plywood walls, stripped t-bolt holds, greasy shoe smears.

I hid instinctively from men I didn't trust in the backroom of bent fixt gears and daisy-chained crusted ropes, skeins of rainbow tape and dried sharpies, color coded buckets of molded plastic holds, all under a layer of fine chalk.

Pigeonholed shoes gone floppy without the feet in them. Muffled acid. Dolly on the aux, a vibe hung drifting like so much chalk dust.

Every week we went through four cans of a sanitizing spray so strong we were supposed to wear gloves with, but we knew it could not kill what was coming.

I wrote *be back march 19th* in fat sharpie and taped it to the desk so white you could run a finger through it.

I hope you understand, the climbers all wore the same tie dye shirt from a pizza place in kentucky and you never seen so many ironic Carhartts.

Can I borrow your clippers, they ask, all dining-hall vegan-skinny, and trim their toenails in broad fluorescent daylight, jam their feet into ballerina pivot points.

I took my feet from the desk only for the flutter of stomach of a body falling to the crash pads.

The climbers will themselves to move, flow skyward, slow against the pull of earth, but always drop back toward the bunker.

Somebody has to vacuum up all that dust.

love poem, revised

Ok so here's what I'm thinking. Knoxville seems like a really good place to be right now. It's pretty deserted which is good and the stores are still good and I've learned a lot since I've seen you last and there are a bunch of cool places around here I'd love to show you. Our cases actually went down by half lol from two to one since someone went back home. I know it's a lot of gas but how would you feel about coming up here for a bit like before they close the borders and shut everything down and we all die? Lol gas is cheap now anyways and like I'd have to take a few days here and there to write some papers etc maybe or just drop out i guess but beyond that it's perfect paddling weather and there's plenty of parking in the fort now. I know rafting season is maybe starting up soon so if you wanna time it out for guide training that could be cool too. Like neither of us have jobs and I know your family is probably worried sick down there so it is a big ask but like I said I've got plenty of rice and beans and tp and you're

welcome to stay here as long as you want. It is
warmish and the mountains are right here and
the boys miss you and I love you. Please come
back to me I've been waiting for you all winter
and there's no one else I'd rather ride out the
end of the world with. I am so full of hope.

Revised:

Ok so I know
it's a whole lot of gas but
how would you feel about coming
up here for a bit? Knoxville seems
like a really good place to be rn
and there's a lot of cool places around here
I'd love to show ya

Revised:

Come back to me. I love you.

Pando

This one time, I saw somebody naked
dimpled marble under David's thumb
stubble and worry lines and crusted eyelids.

This one time, I let somebody
warm his fingers on my shower-damp skin
through our own particular apocalypse.

This one time, we drove to Colorado, stopped for
Pando, the largest organism. Hibernal aspens on
an unassuming hillside: A gathering of roots into
grove as we are a gathering of atoms into body,
as we were a gathering of memories into
synapse, buried under thigh deep snow.

Every large thing is made up of
smaller things, spinning away
from each other, turning and turning.

Wherever he is, the sun rises earlier.
Wind blows fine sand into glittering patterns,
thick rubber dimples ice, steams breath from
our wasted fires.

This one time, I lay on top of him, weighted
blanket, limb for limb, timed my breaths to his.
Lines of blinkers at a stoplight.
My toes curl frozen in his long socks.
He cantilevers off half a mattress, panting.

This one time, he warmed his fingers in my
armpits, passed whiskey in a tin cup, palmed
frost onto my burning core. I was the ice under
his tires. Burn rubber for me, baby. Sleep with a
box fan and burn with a greasy smoke.

This one time, I held frozen peas to my
bellybutton vagus nerve. His nose bled into our
mattress, rinsed again with ice water.
Augured fish cracked through the frozen lake.
Throw it all on the burn pile.

We touched both oceans together – who gets
the pinpricked map? Who keeps the feather jar?
Who will I sit in the god-rays with, watch
water scoop out granite potholes? Who will I
turn to when the cormorant dives, when
the salamander wrinkles, when bark unpeels
and shears down the mountainside?
Into whom will I whisper look?

Whose morning breath sinkhole can I fall into,
whose tongue/hips/fever brain should I
memorize the topography of?

Kite Strings

Since you left I have been touched in new ways.
I have been lifted up by the jaw bone, horse to bridle.
I have heard seashell resonance in his calloused
whorls, his thumb where my ear meets cheekbone.

He is the keeper of a busy dog.
I double dutch the kite strings of his long lead,
adjust my corporeal geometry to different planes,
pattern my murmurs to new frequencies.

Am I the kite or the wind that blows it?
Is he the string or the flier or the sky behind?
In this sense, who is the key or the lightning bolt
or the ground to which it returns?

He's a lefty, red hair and blue eyes.
He says this means he'll live forever,
but I dreamt toxic fumes crested the ridgeline
and no one would let me into the bunker.

I dreamt he was there, in a white suit chased by a
smudge of darkness, new shoes squeaking.
Next time we'll synchronize our watches.

Nothing changed when we saw the murmuration.
You said there's a part in the movie where the birds
move in a cyclone, a great mass of whirling birds,
turning and turning, no sound but wings.
Bad luck to kill a seabird.

Am I the fragile pansies or the sheet that
covers them? Who is the gardener or the frost
that seeps from the ground? If this isn't God's
country why's the sky Carolina blue?

He says *whatcha thinkin.*

I want him like the brittlest of microplastics, floating
bleached on all tides. Eventually, we must recross our
own footprints, notwithstanding that the wind
reshapes the dunes.

Pattern Recognition

One of the jobs of the human brain
is pattern recognition.

If I look down, each clover
has four leaves and each flower
is this big, the color of flame
held behind eyelids.

And if I look up, each car
sputters with your rhythms
and the water folds
back over on itself

And if I look down, there is
my body, my body.
My body. Surely you see it too.

And if I look up, the light
is green, it was never
winter, and we breathe
in the freshest of airs.

Analocisms

Among mature Eastern Hemlocks[7] that hold
dominion over Gatlinburg, Tennessee, there
encroaches the woolly adelgid[8] a small insect
that feeds on the sap at the base of hemlock
needles, which, having starved the mighty
hemlock of her own nutrients, deprives
salamanders, brook trout, and other
cool-stream-dependant species of their habitats.
The woolly adelgid is a textbook invasive
species, someone who does not belong.

---

[7] Lumberjack Mini Golf, Black Bear Pancakes, Dolly Parton's
Dixie Stampede (recently renamed Stampede), Ole Smokey
Moonshine Distillery, Biblical Times Dinner Theater
[8] Jurassic Park minigolf, Live Gators and Sharks, Jimmy
Buffett's Margaritaville Resort, Funky Budha Indian Cuisine

Pigeon Forge, Tennessee

I. Eastern Hemlocks

Among mature giants of Pigeon Forge, regal
since before the first chunk of iron was smelted,
since before first crust of ore was broken from
the mountain, since before last hardwoods were
clearcut, earmarked for tunnel crossbars, the
woolly adelgid beetle, native to Japan, feasts.

Hemlocks, prickling Smokies for millennia, have
learned to live with 30 species of salamander,
hundreds of fish, one bear.
Not humans or bugs they bring.

The beetles starve them, leaving ashen
pockmarks on mountains, radiating islands of
death for 30 dependent species of salamander,
hundreds of fish, one bear.
Eventually humans and bugs they bring.

II. Ginkgos

Pigeon Forgers bemoan their concreted
strip malls, beg for sidewalk
beautification half a mile from
the most biodiverse place in our world.

Think of the leaves! All that beautiful
yellow! And so easy to maintain!
All the tourists who will help us!
Buy our pancakes! Spend nights
 in our hotels! Think of all the people
who will visit our park!

City planners listen to the people,
order 200 female trees on sale
from Japan, to be shipped in next
week, just in time for fall. They are
unaware of the ginkgo fruit's putrescence,
rotten cheese curdled to ward off
predators that died out before dinosaurs.

Every fall, 200 ginkgos drop
all their leaves at once,
miracle orchestrated by oldest gods.

Their fruits, inedible to anything
of this hemisphere, drop too,
squashed by families tripping
to Dollywood, ground, reeking,
into the sidewalks.

Love Boat
Nolichucky River, Erwin TN

You know, they say canoes are divorce boats.
But rafts, rafts are love boats.

To be with him is to rain dance for Spruce Pines,
watch colors move golden up the gorge, skim
pollen from the lake, to put all my shedding skin
to the wind and sundance for technicolor
springtime.

To be with him is to ask on which beach we will
unspool our neoprene, to dream of tomatoes so
ripe their skin falls away when I pick them.

To be with him is to catch surf, clamp saddle
with thigh meat, ride the very instant Poseidon
made horse from foampile, to buck as if the jaws
were biting.

To be with him is to leach mildew sweat into
cedar humidity, laugh fit to burn my nosehairs,
to trust that this time, everything works out.

To be with him is skipped CDs and garbled
phonecalls, static in time to *I want I want I want.*

To be with him is to know precisely the
placement of my organs: If I had feet, I would be
swept off em, breath held, into a river so sweet it
must be bad for you.

To be with him is to clack helmets, pivot the
weight of each other through time.

Fiery Gizzard Collection

Ranks of gray subarus
What are y'all hopping on?

In search of small mosses
Rhododendron
oyster mushrooms layered in frost

Anticline fold
Bearspray and budding briers
A clogged and dripping stove
What is going on

Sandstone teeth worn on recirculating currents
ridgelines of eastern short leaf pines
Hemlocks rib low gorges
Limestone swiss cheese

Red headlamp aimed at Scipio
somewhere in the star book

Pinched hip crests and raw collarbones,
blood coursing in my own two ears.
What happens after this girl?

Plateau rock hops,
half a Newport
A snorting, besweatered bulldog

Bury my presentable half,
give my legs to the worms,
shoot my massive cock up to outer space.

Faith is an encounter with
a power we cannot control.

Pieces of water falling at fifteen frames a second.
Watch it drop, then watch the world go WHOOM

My gizzard is fired indeed.

Kickball / Tomahawk Rock

We went up to moonlit Tomahawk
Rock, granite-pebbled escarpment
as the rind of sun slipped under the valley.
She's got the twang, hair whipping
in the bed of the Ranger.

We spill our dark beers, point at each satellite,
project red-green flashed collisions, measure
Orion's dong by space debris left between stars.
Road rash and a warm tongue moving.
Whatcha thinkin bout? You, only you.

You were busy skating, being driven nuts.
We mime compressions on the same mannequin.
Glasses down my nose, I whisper to thirty.
Webbed Elbows, I have called less than this love.

Later, in my field, a man squats on heel wedges,
explains how to lengthen my eccentric tendons.
A dry-headed man explains how to move my

own body through the water I inhabit.
A man with spiderwebs gathered onto his elbows
explains why he doesn't like to share you.

One of these I asked for.
The Russians, the Chinese, and Left Right Left.
Do better. Piss into the trees.

I smell like pine and a well-used kitchen.
If I slice into the fescue I can plant alfalfa hay
where my cousins sink the golf cart to its axles.

Unlike the cowboy movie, I lay no
claim to the shine in your eyes.

I wish the gold in the hills would stay put,
unmarred by mattock or the explanations

of men, and the deer would come
back to frolic across the frame.

I watch you pitch between anthills
until a loose dogbite punctures my kickball.

Not your *Nectar*
Italics from Nick

It *is only* a figment of your imagination.
natural (whatever that means) women do not
want this.

To cleanse yourself of this desire, you must
want to leave the wine corked, safe inside its
dimmed bottle,

taste only the iron filings of your own mouth,
skin left unbroken.

To Katie

Honey, wrap me
in your mauve puffy jacket, whisper our name
into my ear, whirl me from
this two-dollar Squires wine-fog, leg-wrestle me
on our living-room dumpster carpet,
pin me underneath you,
sing me awake.

Jane Doe

I bite my nails, chew on my pen ends. I'm told
these are anxious habits. I have grooved
my own bottom-front teeth, worn through the soles
of my retainers, changed the shape of my very jaw.

I am told I will be identifiable bleached and mounted.
I am told even strange quarks, the smallest of us,
spin through their chambers in pairs
I am told observation changes the experiment.

Ask the doe how her posture shifts at wolf breath.
I am told of objective truth, void of all
sullied-body subjectivity. Ask the doe why her
flesh is vulnerable to the rending of teeth.

I am told, in great detail, of both the delights
and limitations of my own body, gamey stew.
Ask the doe if she can fathom vegetarian wolves.

I'm told it's only natural to flinch
at hurtled highbeams, but if I could
I would melt dappled
back into second growth rhododendron

I am told I am a prey animal, destined to be caught
by neck or ring finger and brought down.

Poem in the style of *The New Yorker*

When we are out walking in early summer, from
a certain bar to a certain apartment, my lover,
who seeks his fortune as a landscaper, lets go my
small hand to stop and pluck each weed from
the sidewalk cracks and borders. Each time, he
apologizes for the habit, flicks the sprigs into
traffic, and says *if you get them young, they don't
have a chance to establish.* I had been attracted to
his tan and broad forearms, his body's firm
solidity so antithetical to my previous lover's
affectated, tweedy slenderness. I am a writer, by
nature and craft, and in the sunny mornings my
lover takes the origami boulders from my
typewriter wastebasket and refolds them into
intricate flowers without pausing to read the
words veining up the petals. He smuggles me
rogue blooms from other peoples plantings,
murmurs that he watered, fertilized, plucked the
best roses for me. In the end, I was loathe to
begrudge any green thing, resented the pruning
and shaping of my world.

Untitled: no

She said
on the way back from the beach,
he asked for road head
she gagged up 75
as sand baked back to red clay

He said
it's your turn and she said
no that's ok
you don't have to do that.

But he said
I want to

in his tinted too-much-truck
Ac on sunburns
up shimmer ribbon
peppered with state troopers

she said
no
that's ok
you don't have to do that

if you're keeping score at home
that's twice now she's said
no
that's ok
you don't
have
to do that

but he said I want to
and did it anyways.

she said I kept my sunglasses on so he wouldn't
see me cry
through alabama-bright pine barrens
rumblestrips printed on her temples

Later, he said let me make you dinner
and I said no
that's okay you don't have to do that
But he did anyways.

He said I don't think I did anything wrong.
They never do.

He said she has such a negativity in her
such a bitterness
I don't think she was ready
for the love I had for her.

Later, he pulled me up by the scruff of my neck
stuck his tongue so far down my throat I
couldn't say
no that's ok you don't have to do that

he said do you want me to leave
I wiped his spit on my sweatshirt rim
confused by my own secretions
I said no
That's ok
you don't have to do that
But he left anyways

Later, he sat me down by a waterfall
said can I hold you
I said no
that's okay
you don't have to do That

hiked in silence to the trailhead,
thumb on my bear spray trigger
I said this is for you.

I should have said
Can you hold me with a soft mouth
Like a golden retriever with an egg
Can you hold me like warm breath
Underwater
roach puff inside your chest

Can you hold me like my hot pink singing bullet
from Walgreens in broad daylight
like I held eye contact with the cashier
He said
can I get you a bag

i said
no that's ok you don't have to do that

to paunch pushing against polo
walkie talkie clipped to khakis

he said have a nice evening
And I said thank you I will every time
I've said no I meant it.

Kitty Kat
after Josh

Let me come to you in my own
special way, skittish and moon-eyed,
downy fur goosebumped on end.
Why do I find it hard to trust? A heldover
ancestral memory from desert prides of
savannahed women left to sharpen
their own claws. Apex-queens hunted,
domesticated trophy-wives.

Let my tentative nosing smudge your coffee
table, just out of your heavy-handed reach,
gone as soon as you call for me.
Call me stubborn, headstrong and spiteful.
Leave me to my own devices, hiding curled
in your dusty bookshelves.

Put up with my fevered, nocturnal pacing,
paired with inconvenient naps.
Stop trying to explain sensible sleeping habits
to me, void-ruler of self-destructive chaos.

Am I best left outside? Would you like it
if I roamed the neighborhood, brought you
a dead bird? Or must I be apartment-cloistered,
stuck in Netflix cuddle purgatory?

I surrender to your human warmth,
arch my back, trace love-scratches
up your calves, whisker-breathe
right into your nose, bathe myself
for hours after we touch, cleanse myself of
imagined grime in your air-conditioned hell.

Am I too wild for my own good?
Upsetting your dinner plans, yakking
Malibu-drunk on your careful beige carpet.
I want to be able to love you.

Do you understand me when I yowl?
Who do you see shining out of
my crescent-eyes?

Sonnet +1 for Fake Spring

Butyl acrylate, vinyl chloride gas
First fake spring, cattywompous daffodils
I can't stop lisnin to tropical jazz
They're here before their time, says my dentist.

Airborne Toxic Event, Norfolk Southern.
Lost 30 dollars on the Eagles' squares
You ever thought about your face when you cum?
Germinating cow shit, first earthworms.

How dare you think you know better than this?
Distressed denim and two French Toast specials.
Food comes from the whole earth: desert offgas.
Shoplift your dog food, Fellowship of the Ring.

This time I mean it, the world is ending.
She comes in her own time, this is the real spring.

Easter

Me and my sister hide our goosebumps under
sundresses, ankle-lace socks rumpled into keds,
the new whiteness of old navy cardigans.
We never remember the holy morning cold.

We pick Mamaw's irises, stole-purple
perennials to fill the chickenwire cross.

We sit silent as the sun rises through the trees.
Then a quavering, simple hymn,
coffee and donuts.

On our way to Grandma's, we gorge ourselves
on pastel m&ms still tangled in plastic grass,
grow carsick on Central time.

The Movable Feast spread on pollen-covered
patio chairs: cold ham, slaws, salads loosely
defined wilt in their own mayonnaise.

White Noise
Sequoyah Hills, Knoxville

Listen to the Prius whirr, turning sharklike
from gated driveway.
Listen to the lawnmower churn diamond swaths
Listen to the hum of bicyclists, pod of fish roving

Listen to silver-dollar gravel crunch
under her neon rubber sneakers, skid
over itself, displaced by her doe-prancing jog.

Listen to her tennis skirt swish, scalloped
white hem chafe sculpted thigh, browned
by hissing midMarch spraytan.

Listen to the muffled Harry Styles bleed
from her airpods, a syrup chorus
tinny in the empty, curated air.

Listen to the Method lemongrass soap waft
from her wrists and palms and fingers.
Listen to the trees rustle, bought
and planted and placarded *in honor of.*

To Persephone

I knew you grew from the blood Apollo spilled.
When we first met, you were in full bloom,
trapped under the skin of sun,
heat and wind in your eyes.

Easy laughter, sweaty and sunburnt and loud.
You are not the earth or the sky,
but all that between which is human.
I know you are my summer house.

Drink as your Sunday sets,
drink before Hades sets your Monday alarm.
Let me bask in your refracted moon-rays.
Seasons are changing because he is here.

I love you.
I am ready to throw up.
But with his help, you leave,
return to the dead land in the west.
For the first time, the air is cold.

The frozen Styx still turns.
You leave and the earth dies.
It would not be hard to die.
Leave me here to draw in on myself.
I will let you go into the ground.

How to roll a kayak

Grow up ten miles from home, Ocoee.

Watch kayakers swivel, whirled candy.

Let someone hold your boat, then hold you.

Listen when she tells you to push
your left elbow down, arch your spine.

Pull the boat back under you.

Wash the chlorine from your nose.

Keep time on the warmth you can see rising,
exultant from her clean streamline.

Forward Two
Ocoee, Tennessee

I have felt earth's center pivot under breakers of
second-changing tides. Nice and easy, forward
two. Nobody knows who the pandabear shoots.
Weight the raft on water over rock. Everyone
laughs at her. Forward two.

For I am used to weighted water on top of me.
Short-ended lever, bend always downhill. Follow
the path of least resistance. I have felt my own
insignificance at industrial buoyancy. Nobody
knows the pirate's pants. Weight in raft on rocks
underwater. Forward two more.

I have yanked chicken strap like wet corset
strings or the collar of a dog. Twelve hunnert
cubic feet per second of dynamic force.
Everybody, forward two.

I have felt caught edge cataclysm, held surf as
strangers spilled over my tubes. My own
whiplashed bodies bob in anonymous jackets,

slap at water, bump along rocks. Everyone
laughs at her. I have held my breath longer than
you. Thin scrim above sharp algae. The
unknownness of my needs frightens me.
Forward two more.

I have watched nested copperheads writhe
under man made rock. I have watched men make
the rock from quikrete and river in five gallon
buckets, cement to hold against the water.
I have seen comical physics caught on tape,
drowned punchlines in wavetrains. I have
gnarled my knuckles and pulled my back
muscles. Everybody give me two more.

I have watched men turn the water on,
thundered gently over correct dam, misted onto
camera lenses. I have watched men turn the
water off again, pond scum steaming in sun.

I have been short ended lever wedged against
gravity, snorted not earth from my nostrils down
my own red jacket. I have seen the sun take up
residence, patterned on the skins of those I love.

Nobody knows the genie's wish. I have smelled
night beers seep through pores of different
skins. I have never seen surface from bed but
kick blind, hand above paddle, grab liquid space
between aerations. Everybody get down.

I have set both hands on chicken strap, hauled
myself in, my own dead fish. The rest come in
by their lapels, drip, avoid eye contact. Everyone
laughs, viking warship or drunken spider. I've
felt my own bones pull away from each other.
Tendons protesting the swing of the pendulum
carved through currents pounding from sand
gate spillway. All together: forward two more.

Sometimes, it works. We glide light through gate
rocks and the breeze blows hair away from our
faces. Sometimes girl scouts land clattering
backflips, squeal in bright sun. Sometimes my
voice is gone. I yell anyway, grin at helmet backs.
If you pee right in the water, nobody will know,
but they will laugh all the same.

Chilhowee, Obliterated

I.

sunburn peeling from your nose is
    the pink of a Naturdays can,
      first chancing sunset,
      shadow of a Tinder flame

sunshine stored in your tangled ends is
    the yellow of a Twisted Teas box and
    nothing else,
      first morning through Melissa's windows
      self-conscious laughter

spangle of freckles meeting your underbelly is
    the tan of rain-gorged Ocoee, beigeing
    into whitenoise,
      dark smell of boulders sweating under
      mountain laurels,
      warmth of skin on skin on skin on skin

center of your level eyes is
    the blue of a Quest paddle head,
    flooded Parksville dining rooms,
    Chilhowee after seven

II.

The sun is setting on your day.
The mistake can be traced
to the first sentence:
O.

The day was almost over.
Outside, open the box where it is:
you're locked out. In her windows,
laugh together.

Oil samples are collected below
in blackness, burn beige-white;
Deep peaks at the feet of mountains
warm the skin.

You have your time.
Chilhowee rises seven times later.

III.

The sun is out from behind your nose.
It can be tricky to write the first verse
of a living shadow.

The sun is at its end.
Outside, open something else,
outside yourself. In her window,
it was a laugh together.

Volumes of oil were collected under
dark colors, beige to acrid white;
depths of rocks below the mountains,
heat the skin to the skin.

Your time is your priority.
Chilhowee moves behind all seven.

IV.

Your sun sets on our last day.
Trace time back to my first thought,
of you on my porch.
O, you are smaller than you looked
on Tinder.

Our day was not almost over.
Open my box where it sits
on the bottom of Parksville lake.
You're locked out
of our last laugh.

Collect mushrooms in nail clipping moonlight.
In blackness, burn beige-white.
Breathe in the skin I left on your sheets.
Deep peaks at the feet of mountains
warm the skin.

You have your time.
The moon rises behind Chilhowee over and over.

Charlie's Bunion

Swaddled in your yellow tent, blended so
tightly with the finally golden leaves,
I unkink my cramped hips, swivel to your
eleven-in-the-morning soft-warm breath.

After our last time with a guru, we spool out
another episode, alone. Yellow melts to red in
the same places as my favorite body. The only
part that lasts: red sun behind your eyelids.

Mumbled g'mornings, still-zipped sleeping bags,
The Grapes of Wrath left crinkled and undone.
Ask how you slept, if I need anything,
if I want you to start the oatmeal soon.

Most of the time, your hand is around my neck.
It was eleven in the morning, hot. We pack away
sleeping boxes for the southern winters. Rats
clean, eat infected ones. So you left the Lord to
seek the truth, if nothing else.

Pull me in! Stay in Tennessee, endure
the cold against your nature. Stay and I'll
huff my breath onto your frosted windows.

If you want to, if you're ready, start with fat, trim
yourself. Why? Draw an account of yourself in a
natural environment. Count your footprints. Say
Look, I was here. Correct your periscopic,
timelapsing window.

I'm counting down to the first snow, mapping
the miles to Colorado, telling my friends we've
parted ways, holding you tighter.

Scooby Snacks

Returning flushed from Colorado highlands,
wind-burned, coughing out hazy
mountain air you come, back bent under
the weight of secret riches.

You pull out a quart- nay!- a gallon
ziploc bag, forget to weigh it, rapture in the
fresh, money- green smell of summer petrichor.

You cook bushels of applesauce, pass
trays of brownies around. You give away
everything you love, friends come
easy, and life in the South isn't hard.

You've lost chairlift-equipped alpine slopes, but
the rivers, the rivers let you cum
quietly on their hospitable tiddies.

You whittle 2 for .99 Swishers, don't care who
pulls their lawnchair up to the fire-ring.

But your stash starts fading,
lost in a summer of unripe blooms,
nectar too stubborn to recognize its own use.

You tap-sift ashes, uncrinkle sharpie-labeled
ziplocs, scrape them inside out.

You turn to pitiful gatorade contraptions,
something sticky melted in the July
dryness onto something else.

Something sprouts alone,
hidden behind car tires.

Grayson Highlands, or Turning 20

the milky way gyres above you for the first time,
cocooned within your rented turquoise shell,
bracketed by Margie and sweet, sweet Mason.

let the clouds dust you with dew, time your rise
to the breakfast-bell moos and reckless
blackbird susurrus, offer feral tongues your
sweat-salted arm.

air out the car on the way home, glimpse Jackie
drowsing in the rearview mirror as Aidan runs
out of playlists, his Pennsylvania-Scotch
murmurs threading down I-81.

shiver in cracker barrel still packed with diabetic
churchgoers on Monday afternoon, mutter,
resentful and starved.

eat five biscuits waiting, spoon
strawberry jam, guzzle sweet tea,
remain hungry.

Patina

Each bee I've seen lately is different,
crossbred hornets with toned hulls and harsher
stripes, wings with new patterns in their folding.

Each orange I peel has not seeds but polyps,
Strange growths in the crook of each pod,
And the weather is not what was predicted.

They tell me a war has kicked up again, show me
fireballs like dust devils across the highway.
They say this knowledge is a privilege.

I see hemlock skeletons in each forest,
and kudzu overtaking farmhouses.
This too is change.

Under the marble, beneath each fold of toga,
there is skin spilling over,
broken and worn to the taste of a body.

Each chip from my paddle is memory
cured in harbor-freight epoxy.

Turned leaves float downstream,
ribbons of my own hull on each rock.

At home, my kitchen table is stained with
oobleck, smeared sticky with jam and beer,
and I trace each of your hard-smiled wrinkles.

Cleaning House
a breakup ghazal

Hork your hairballs from the showerdrain of my self.
Swab morningbreath spit from the sinkmouth of my self.

Toss your moldy chicken burritos from my whining fridge.
Buff your forkscratches from the nonstick pan of my self.

Water my neglected kitchen-sill succulents. Soak crusted
casseroles in steaming Dawn, burning myself.

Tidepen sweatstains and bodyheat from my comforter.
Wash my pillowcases of sour tears cried all by myself.

Restack the books on my floor, but leave your
birthday-gifted pocketknife by my bedside, guess since
you're gone I do need to protect myself.

Crack windows, light candles to cauterize your weed-funk.
Burn some sage too, just in case I'm haunting myself.

Channel ancestral Scottish mothers, keening for your
absence. Bleed out maxipads worth of whatever residue
you left inside my self.

Applesauce

Give me your nasty apples.
Set your soggy box on my doorstep.

Give me your number. Let me scoop up
your rottenness, cook you down
into something better.

Let putrid juice leak from your seams,
ambrosia for neighboring raccoons.

Come over, come in. Leave
sticky smears along my hallway walls.

Get me the peeler from the drawer by the sink,
clear laptops and ashtrays from the kitchen
table.

Let my fingers sink into your tired thighs,
peel off your jeans to get at the core of you.

Let your fingers sink into mushy brown spots,
thumb off stubborn produce stickers.
Drop fragrant peels into our compost bucket.

        Let me pare out the best parts of your
          insides, reclaim you from the landfill,
            make you sweet and soft.

Leave your seeds in, poison for everyone I love.
Dump your soggy pieces into our biggest pot.

      Let your most human drizzle pool onto my
        spoon. Burn my tongue, let me taste
          metal and overwhelming earth.

Let the apples simmer in their own blood, add
the last of the sugar. Forget to stir.
Let them smoke, burnt-carmel.

Let your pectin set overnight, slowly
congealing. Fall asleep on my couch,
mold your rhythms onto my own.

Get me the big bowl, help me strain out two
gallons of what has finally become applesauce.

Let me ladle you into mason jars, bring you to
potlucks, devour your stewed and pulpy body
with everyone I love.

Let the big pot sit on the stove all week,
domesticity too exhausted to do the dishes.

Let my text sit unread, exhausted
heart resigned again to trawling Tinder.

Pillars of Creation

I'm thinking of Utah, the last winter my body
twined around a stranger's, of red rocks,
fantastic piles, sandstone castles crumbled
under oiled fingerprints.

I'm thinking of night frost in the Mars-red
desert, winds playing over the sand, stars
patterned after my own breath, of how
even then I couldn't speak to anyone, skittish
of the breaths of strange cosmonauts,
safe in the van and its rocking.

I'm thinking of the Salton Sea, the glare of
California, wet wiping tacky grit in parking lots,
the people who carried their homes as we did,
so much space junk, so many plywood boards
sprayed with NEED DOG FOOD AND WEED.

I'm thinking of a candle velcroed to the inverter
box, of Thanksgiving on a picnic table, instant
potatoes and boxed stuffing on the camp stove.

Whenever I shiver at night I think
of you, kneeling at the propane
heater, sure it would kill you.

I'm thinking of how far I would've made it alone.
But here I am, again in that dust-cloud, watching
leaves change, strange breaths in my bed.

Here I am again, calling him Pumpkin, watching
another dog run across my yard, telling myself
this time will be different, is already different,
twitch-breath as he swirls his fingers around the
hole someone made in me.

At the wedding, the minister read of Adam's rib,
the deep sleep, then its plucking. He said woman
was taken from man, to be his companion,
and that man is not meant to be alone.

Here I am, with sand between my toes still,
mapping out another canyon.

The Lighthouse

On our first night at the post, I shovel piles of black
coals in the hungering fire,
feeding the foghorn's siren sound.
That's alright sir, I don't drink
liquor anymore, not since Winslow drowned in the sea
of timber last winter, haunting my nightmares with fog.

Our shaft of light pierces the morning fog
so I know a storm is coming, black
clouds roll in over the doldrummed sea.
I watch as you light a fire
in your belly, ward off the dropping barometer with drink.
Your off-key sailor-ballads keep time with foghorn sound.

You say there's a soul trapped in this gull, but the sound
of its cawing accuses me endlessly over the fog-
crusted beach. I drink
in the silence as its cold, black
blood seeps onto blacker rocks. You threaten to fire
me for bringing bad luck, but who will care? Only the sea.

I think I spot a siren far out to sea
the pitiful sound
of her cries lighting a fire
in my lonesome loins. Breathing out fog,
she warns us of the storm, dips back down into the black
waves. I shiver, take another drink.

Marooned on this godforsaken rock, we run out of drink
and chug precious lamp-oil, leave the sea
to light herself, let black
Triton's anger thunder on, his sound
buried under our desperate singing, the fog
of our drunkenness interrupted only by lightning-fire.

I want to see what you are keeping in your tower, the fire
that powers our light. Asleep from the last of the drink,
I steal your keys and sprint through the fog.
I try to bury you, but you won't rest away from the sea.
My footsteps on the salty iron stairs resound.
I stare into the sun of the light. Everything grains to black.

The concentrated fire of our light moves slow over the sea.
Our relief drinks the sound of feeding gulls. Siren-cries
through fog, our bodies spots of white heat in blackness.

Blackwater
Suwannee River

Come back to the land of the living
from the cracks you know too much of:
nurses who call you by name,
bedrails, paper sheets, and stiff-chaired dreams.
An unawakening.

I lit a candle for you, as I always do, in my attics
and behind my bookshelves. I dreamt of a yellow
quilt, haunted by the pattern sewn for me.

Come back into summertime, perfect sunshine,
where we'll fill the mosquitoes to bursting.

Pack your glass in ghost bags, your spirit in
layers of grit, sticky peat and sweet seafoam.
Tell your dog what he's about to do,
croon as he whines in my ear.

String up with me in the live oak wallow,
pruned fingers, spring-fed eyes, wrinkled
pages by one headlamp.

Know that each place has its own ferryman, its
Sasquatch stair guardian. Each truth is
subjective, and everywhere is change.

Watch acid etch holes into limestone coral
bones, knobbed gators sink into blackwater,
cypress-tannin tea-stained, thousand-wake of
well-fed vultures, mirror-breaking manatee
snout, motel floor and gnat-dancing.

I dreamt the ghost-witch in my crawlspace
kidnapped your dog, scratched her fingernails in
his fur, and nibbled the ticks from his ears, as I
walked through an old house, all mine, all alone.

Listen for silent carillon, haunted rangers in
abandoned camps, hurricane-wrecked staircase
creaking, the whispered catching of current.

Feel my skin between your teeth.
Come back to the land of the living.

black cat, running across a football field

A piece of shadow
skims across the astroturf,
puffed up, hissing in
the end zone, touchdown Cowboys.
MetLife stadium erupts.

Monday Night Football
now consumes internet teens.
The cat is a meme.
Perhaps he'll be adopted
with his celebrity clout.

He is named, known, but
given less space to run in.
He gains weight, while rats
and pigeons breed in MetLife.
The field is covered in poop.

Tension Dial

You want to hit the sweet spot. Turn the knob
somewhere tighter than a 2, which makes the
back of your piece into the loopy scrawl that
your seventh grade social studies teacher
refused to grade, that your first boyfriend is
disappointed by. He thought your hands would
write neater, nicer.

But somewhere looser than a 3, which puckers
your piece into your mother's mouth in the
fitting room, *well you need something, Katherine*
arcing through your twelve year old brain.

You've gotta feel it, the sweet, churning clatter
of work being made, in your cramping palms and
pincushioned fingers, in your thread-dusted lap.
Hunch over the table of scattered notions,
scrapped dreams.

Make something known and understood as
woman, leave out the darts for where your boobs
should go.

Gingerbread

I live in the valley where life once formed, where
the ground is not sand but muck: deep clay fit
for sculpting voodoo dolls, funerary urns, and
lake bottoms. Where eyes peek from strata and
christmas is lit with antiquated incandescence,
where the only outlet spins *blue christmas*, very
scratched, treasured as a first, only snow.

We are custodians of our own etched, tactile
artifacts, attics of cookbooks, garages of bibles,
hidden brailled deep from amalgamated
datasets. What gets left behind?
Everything changes.
Everything passes away: dams crumble into that
same clay, candles melt inside gingerbread
golems of butter, sugar, spice.

In this, our clay, there are no places to hide.
When I buy butter, sugar, spice, I must ask the
robot how to make a man, how long to bake him,
since I have forgotten, or was never taught, and
then she sells me heavy cream and all the rest:
candles and streamers and tinsel.

We always stop halfway, on the ridge that marks
the stateline, where the booths have time limits,
where the bathroom camera fluorescence angles
up inside me, which is normal, where I am no
longer proud of the things my body can do,
greased and folding like dough.

I would never think myself worth anything other
than this clay, any harder stones or steaks
better-formed than catfish, than your itchy dog
or three tires full.

There are places where the silt piles up and the
lake bed dries and cracks in the sun, the fish
gasping, where you can count every tree on your
acreage, land that belongs to you, brush your
fingers along rock, hide from her satellite
thermal imaging in grooved and pockmarked
ground.

Here, where the land was sea and then mountain
and then lake and now you, and anyone left to
listen to your music.

None of these mistakes kills you, until one does.
Each zillow listing expires.
Everything changes,
everything passes away.

the robot

I. Dashing

How do I tell you what I do? How most days the
robot in space pilots my hamster car, watches
me move through a strange town?

I tell each visored teenager your name, which
the robot told me, and they hand me a wrapped
sack of only smells. If I'm lucky, the robot
glitches and the stickers sweat off greasy paper,
unwrapping your luxury, short-circuiting your
comfort. I nibble your breadsticks and
frenchfries, sip your corn syrup tamarind and
turquoise Baja.

How do I tell her I can't see in darkness?
How do I tell her what a mistake means?

For the first time, I wish for more asphalt,
pebbled so smooth that the streetlights drip off
it in this, the only rain, low curbs and numbered
houses, ordered bright in the glow of headlights.

II. I've been dreaming of haunted houses.

I've been browsing the listings, looking for
flash-lit crawlspaces, remembering which
houses have Oldsmobiles and wheelchair ramps
and Walgreens deliveries left in piles on porch
rockers. I've been noticing parts of my body
that I swear were never there before, lines and
folds and wrinkles, been trying to tell myself it
doesn't matter, nothing matters. In the house I
dreamt last night, there are reflections, probably
headlights, in the dark-mirrored windowpanes,
and the terror is not of the dark, because what
now is really dark, but of who emerges from the
brown haze, sodium-orange, flickering LED
pierced by fluorescent hibeams. None of this is
pleasant. In another house, my sister knocks
over my christmas tree, my mother lies to me,
my dad gives me an old quilt with stained yellow
batting. And I remember how exhausting it is to
question where everything comes from.

III. the robot

How do I tell her what a mistake means?
How sometimes the marble slips
from its groove and clatters through the
scaffolding, the groan of curbs and sharp
driveways and bumpers not my own.

How do I tell her of the foglights cresting the
hilltop, the crunch of gravel, when she knows
already every time that my heart beats, which
organs I suck in for pictures?

Still there is room for grace, a delay from the
upload to the ping, enough time for me
to angle myself out of frame.

Rarely does a front door open to me, only once
have you called me by name.

The young ones apologize when I pass their
houses, guiding me from space around the bulb
of the cul de sac.

IV. Incarnation

I can't beat the robot. I can take your food and
tell her it wasn't there, never existed. I can tell
her I can't make it up your driveway in the rain.
She has me caught from three different angles,
clearer than the game cameras that watch deer
blue-eyed browsing corn in the night. She knows
the gradient of each driveway already, from
space, but still asks permission to tell me which
ads I prefer. The robot is selling my step count,
profiting from each of my heartbeats.
She doesn't care where the food goes.
Neither of us matter to her.
She doesn't have a body, but if she did it would
be head to toe shrouded in concrete, server
towers stacked and blinking plastics rarer than
gems, hidden in California, or somewhere named
The Cloud, in a bunker, watched herself by
cooling fans. Impossibly wise, terribly young.

Why have we not given her a body?
What happens when she is not just a voice but a
presence?

V. Touch Grass

We look down and watch the tidal waves and
televised insurrections, full of false starts and
waiting. They've changed all the movies on
Netflix, and nothing is the same anymore, the
outside grey and the darkness coming too soon.

We look up, at the clean snap of a dry branch.
We've come this way before, looking for
mushrooms with boys who always go broke
before Christmas. Through the gully on
gametrail, past trash-pile singlewides,
evergreens and leaf mould
and styrofoam pebbles.

Later, I learn of another robot, who is perhaps
related to mine. She tells you which mushrooms
are poisonous, knows your dog and children
from the pictures you've taken of them. What
happens when she's wrong?

We looked up and noticed the Earth had moved. Certain ruins had finally crumbled, and the sun shone from a different place.

We looked down, into each other, and I placed my hand on the top curve of your belly, swirled the red hairs around. It is warm here, the divot in my own mattress, since the dog sleeps on both of our feet. I hear the blood moving inside you, the strange clicks your mouth makes when you sleep.

I am not free as long as one person of color is chained. Nor is any one of you.
     Audre Lorde

Someone has shown me where the chained
people are, how to forge a pickaxe
hypothetically, Netflix documentaries, murder
in 1080p, split and bloodied 60-second stories.
I know, today, exactly where the people are
the ones in actual, physical chains.

I ate Nestle chocolate yesterday, cacao beans
harvested by enslaved people. The coffee I drank
this morning was not certified fair trade. I
scrolled past testimonies from Uighur Muslims
in Chinese concentration camps.

My license plate was stamped out by an unpaid
prisoner with a greater chance of being arrested,
charged with jail time because of his race.
The chip in my phone was made by children
being paid unfair wages, suicide nets in factory
stairwells.

Anavysos Kouros

It is 10:30 on a Tuesday, in HSS 114.
The professor clicks your slide onto the
projector. I am floored, awakened from my
midlecture glazed stare,

enraptured by your vacant almond eyes, blissful
Archaic death-smile, hoplite-trained thighs
sliding gently outward.

And when she flips to the next slide, her velvet
Belgian lisp interprets your curves, your
monumental, colossal, historical significance.

The thiccest ass that could ever be coaxed from
Grecian stone stares me down from the grainy
illumined slide, comfortable, sausage-cased
tendons.

voluptuous marble, welcoming strength,
love me from 2500 years' remove.

OPVS ROMANVM

I. Spotting in the Galleria Borghese

Starched sheets, tight curls. Violent, folding skin.
I've only ever seen this stone on courthouses
and kitchen counters, never like this, shone into
a body. The robot says you, the master, daub the
martyrs with blood so light I can still see the
brushstrokes. The air between your bristles. Let
me show you what nakedness means. My own
lining sink-washed and loose inside me. Let me
show you how to paint with the body. When I
clench too hard I can feel the metal inside me.
Or maybe it's the plastic, copper. Without
pushing myself back into place, there's a
different kind of pain, a sucking absence, and I'm
scared my wires will come loose, get caught.
Rip the lining of my purse away.

I'm thinking of how to say goodbye. Is it any
easier to pull a coat from a chair and slip
through the sliding door than it is to crane my
neck to the ceiling one last time?

To tell everyone I've ever met exactly where it all
went wrong, claiming a weak stomach,
exhaustion?

The waters miss you, each drop.
You are still a part of the stream.

How does the rain work here? When it comes,
what does it mean? There are oranges fruiting in
some sacred grove, and the hawkers hold wool
scarves up to women in peacoats.

After, I have the robot walk me home, showing
me the blue dot of myself moving over seven
ancient hills. She tells me this is a storm. In the
city with all its edges worn smooth, where the
land has never thought of moving. Where the
ground never freezes and any thunderbolt must
be divine. I ask her to play me sounds of the
forest. My own forest. The birds and mists my
robot and I know, in a room with three strangers
who I'm sure are listening to their own music.

II. PETRAS

Here, too, I have noticed the robot.
I visited this basilica the morning after the Pope
did something special. And I watched the men in
uniforms restack the folding chairs onto the
trailer of their golf cart, its tires squeaking on
the marble and its orange domelight strobing off
all the folds in the robes of the statues.

I watched the nuns change the linens on the
altar, unfolding and pulling straight the new
whiteness, crisp as my hostel bedsheet. The
nuns roll out a plastic tablecloth for the candle
drippings, the same way I've put down a towel to
catch my blood, and leave through a door that
blends into the walls, a ramp sloping
downwards. I trip over a wire, climb a curved
and hidden staircase, and notice a woman on a
scaffold with a toothbrush, cleaning the leg of a
cherub, pressed here by someone else's hand
however many years ago.

How much of this don't we see, the conquests
and back exits from tombs? How much has the
robot shown me? How much has God?
Day before yesterday I saw mummies behind
glass, shrunken and wrapped only in linen.
Today, I saw John Paul, or Benedict, the same but
lit brighter, with offering boxes out front.
I listened to a service, what do you call it? Is it
Mass when it's small and on a Monday morning?

All this to say the speakers have been painted to
look like marble, gray and swirled, the voice of
the priests piped through this place that was
barrelvaulted to acoustical perfection by men
with more money than God.

All this to say the tourists hold their robots up to
the gilded ceiling, flashes sparking against the
LEDs, in this place that was built while
Copernicus was saying maybe we are a part of
the universe.

People taking pictures of themselves in sacred places, buying souvenirs with the face of the guy who said *make not my Father's house a house of merchandise*. Is this not the world? Is this not the way it works, having a body in a space? Didn't anyone bring their easels and stone tablets, making portraits in front of all of it?

I'm starting to see the point. All of this is too much. What a horrible place to lie in, to feel guilty and wrong in, to confess before someone who knows everything about you. Can you imagine if these statues stood with one foot stepped forward, hips kicked back, held themselves minimized and flattered?

The tourists ask the robot to tell them where they are. They hold her in front of placards and tap until she reads to them in words they can understand.

All this to say there's a security camera mounted on top of a confessional and something strange given to who I think is St Francis. I'm getting better at saints- Sebastian is the hot one who only ever wears a convenient fold of drapery, Bruno is bald, Jeremiah is skinny, and John the Baptist holds a little dish.

Anyways, the tourists write Francis little notes, fold them on scraps of paper, and throw them at his feet. Some on the backs of receipts with the QR code sticking up. Can God read them, the prayers in binary? Does the robot care to?

III. BOCCA DELLA VERITAS

Here, too, there are eyes blinking. In the crypt of
the emperor, the niches carved from stone that
is itself wearing away, all the relics pillaged and
lost, nevermind the apotropaic gaze, the camera
blinking from above the doorway.
Here, too, a Korean in a sweatsuit takes a
picture, his flash decanting the stairwell
candlelight. He throws a strange coin on the
flagstones and curtseys when he leaves.
This, too, is the world.

Here, the robot says this line is to see an artifact.
She says it's a block of marble, like everything
else in this city, and it's the head of Oceanus, in
relief. He used to either cover a manhole or
catch the blood of bovine sacrifices in some
temple, in the hole of his open mouth. The robot
tells me these people are lining up to stick their
hands inside him. If they are lying, the QR legend
says, he will come to life and bite off their hands.

So they pose, one hand in his mouth, one hand covering theirs, looking surprised. Surely they know he won't bite. Thousands of tourists, with their greasy hands, rubbing and widening the hole. What power have we given him, standing here, bearing witness? And what power have we taken from this god, stilled in the narthex of another? Or are we all truthful now, posing under her eyes? This is all too much. Choral music piped through the wiring, motorbike noises from the street outside. What a horrible place to be wrong in, to be burdened by guilt and grief. I wanted clarity, in the exact place where people have been looking for 2000 years and the best thing they could come up with was piles of marble and a power without a name, a woman and her son painted in gold.

Here, too, there is water falling, and there are the people taking pictures, placing parts of themselves in view of its fall.

IV. Orvieto

Here, too, there is water falling, and there are
the people taking pictures, placing parts of
themselves in view of its fall.

Here, the Italians wear Carhartts and
knockoff Skechers, cowboy boots
and white Nikes.

This nakedness makes me want to run my
tongue up against bronze. Women reduced to
lines opening up, falling away from what has
been taken from them. Their faces in shadow,
under elbows and behind the slope of thighs.
Portraits taken from behind. This in contrast to
the spiralled pillars, the gilt and the robes
flowing, the curls chiselled from marble. The
movement and twisting of rock.

I have eaten sweet pork, new parts of the pig I can now call cinghiale. I have climbed stairs meant for donkeys and emperors, women and cardinals and bellkeepers. Up the insides of domes, through fortifications and down into wells. Thousands of years of footprints behind turnstiles and ticket offices, all in the name of a photo.

I have heard the plop of strange coins into new waters, felt the metal on my tongue, the echo of the splash up the walls. Should I kiss it? Can I watch it? Can you call me over the ocean, listen with me to the static waters, the surging tides, the new pressures on my ears? Listen.

Here too, the chef flirts and mixes with a red kitchenaid, and the children drop their Batmen from highchairs, and the nonnas wear their readers on chains around their necks. This, too, is the world. This is the breaking of fine clay.

The robot shows me a man with his mouth
covered and body obscured. The blur of his face.
He says porcelain shatters glass and throws
saucers through Tesla windows, bipping
backpacks from trunks, the camera shaky as he
runs. What comes next.

An old man tells me he's lived here all his life. He
says there's no crime, and I think how hard it
must be to steal marble, to pick up all of this and
walk away with it. But I remember the women,
Proserpina and Daphne, all the Sabines thrown
over shoulders, reaching and twisting, falling in
place. I remember the pillars in the forum with
the gouges in their flanks, from when peasants
soaked ropes in vinegar and flossed away the
literal pillars of democracy for their precious
white stone.

The old man says there is surveillance everywhere, as a comfort. He takes me to a monument to Sigmund Freud, who stayed here and of whom he is very proud, and points to a camera whose eye is not blinking. The whole time I'm thinking of how to hit him with my bag of apples, positioning myself in anticipation of violence. Nothing happens. He takes me around the charming city, perched so high on its quaint hillside that it's never been taken by force, since Etruscan times, some beautiful woman having offered herself up to the Nazis in exchange for her quaint, charming city.

I'm thinking of what parts women play here, taking Jesus down from the cross and all the rest, tending the bodies and babies and floating around naked with wings on. Snapping and drawing out arrows and posing naked on chilled marble couches.

V. Florence

My bunkmate, a kindergarten teacher in Poland,
tells me of the Florence Effect, *where you are
looking at so much art that your brain goes crazy,*
and in her eyes I see a breathlessness, an energy
sparking from her fingers. Today she went to the
Uffizi and then a perfume store, and this whole
evening she has been breathing deep from the
sample sticks, five little strips of nice paper that
each smell of a different jasmine, trying to
decide.

And from the Wiki, I who must learn, who must
classify, see that Stendhal says
*I was in a sort of ecstasy, from the idea of being in
Florence, close to the great men whose tombs I had
seen. Absorbed in the contemplation of sublime
beauty ... I reached the point where one
encounters celestial sensations ... Everything
spoke so vividly to my soul. Ah, if I could only
forget. I had palpitations of the heart, what in
Berlin they call 'nerves'. Life was drained from me.
I walked with the fear of falling.*

And I thought I was alone here, walking with the fear of falling, neck craned up and tripping over the cobblestones.

And sometimes I wish I could, like Mary does, in one of the thousands of altarpieces, *come down from heaven and into the world of trees, water, and sky.*

At home, I know where the moon is, and am not surprised to see her grow to fullness. Home where the smog smells of leaves, and the ground is soft and changing. Everything is nicer here– the bars on the windows are sturdier and sculpted into faces, the planks are real wood, birch-by-sixes, and all the angles line up. Here, in this place that was for so long fixated on mathematical perfection, on art contoured and sculpted, lines and angles and depth. And I wonder what I am pushing out to keep my mind whole, what am I shoving back into my suitcase, literally walking on graves, the camposanto, filigree inlaid in marble.

What wears me down?
The clatter of scaffolding, pitched almost like
bells, the saints in their niches, their marble
robes draped in plastic sheeting. The crane in
the nave and the crack through the cross in the
cupola, the selfie sticks and metal detectors. The
catacombs and the gift shop, the rosaries for
sale in the crypt. Satellite dishes painted to
match the terracotta roof tiles, curved to the
shape of the maker's thigh. The collection box
that flips a switch to light the chapel, where the
glare reflects off the oils that have been dimmed
by time, that degrade with each exposure to
light. Every so often there is a clank of euros and
a flash, balancing the Nativity that twinkles with
Christmas lights. The power that defies figural
representation, and women with literal wings.
Medusa, screaming and disembodied, painted on
the shield, the whites of her eyes vibrating
under the lights. Bells that weren't meant to be
heard in silence, have always been pitched to
ring through the murmur, the congregation of
people.

Focus on one brushstroke, one pane of glass.
Think of the hands that put it there, the work,
the work. The work. Scaffolding around a tower
that's been falling since before it was finished.
Notice that the tourists are posing to prop up
the tower, not to knock it down. Notice that they
identify all the bones in the reliquaries: tibia,
fibula, teeth. The sauna is cold and the
perfumery is closed, though smells leak from the
doorway. Nothing is as I thought it would be.

Nothing is as I thought it would be, wasting
paper, feeling the waters, finally, hold all of my
skin. Before all of this, I saw the ground open
before me, saw rock sculpted not by two hands,
many hands, but by the breaths of wind and
time. Canyons and arches, buttes and playas, all
of it, too, made by water, however long ago,
coursing over rock.

And once I overheard *jesus christ* on the stairs
up to the museum. Not looking at the painted
wonders, but at the plywood walls of the
renovation, the continual renovation, funded by
the friends, the romans, the countrymen, in this
birthplace of drama, of rebirth. The birthplace of
the rebirth. Come on. And I heard a *see, told you
they didn't have an elevator.* And there I was
thinking how good it feels to have a body, the
power in my thighs pushing against the grooved
basalt, the ancient cement. How good it feels to
move away, to flee from the freezing of stone.
And then, staring into one of the Madonnas
robed in a blue so deep it had just been invented,
after I had stared so hard at so many altarpieces,
my neck and feet and back hurt, since even
when I'm taking breaks on the benches I'm
staring so hard at the ceilings and columns and
portraits and statues. And just today I've seen
more art than I ever have in my entire life
combined, and in this that used to be an office
building, back when rich people paid artists to
make art, if nothing else.

And I stare at the Venus, behind bulletproof
glass, catching the fingerprints and the glares.
Is anything lost when she's seen through glass?
Just today the robot told me someone threw
soup at the Mona Lisa, again. And something
about how art is living, is in dialogue with the
context of the times, and what our contribution
will be, what sashes we'll paint over the genitals
of history. How easy it is to paint over a flag, to
drape fabric or snatches of leather over an
unmoving body.

How easy, to light a torch with your finger, to
blow the clouds away with your breath, to dub
the audioguide into words you understand.
I watch the people taking pictures in front of
her, posing as if they're looking at her, casually,
with glances over their own shoulders, in front
of this woman famed for her vanity, famed for
her gesture at modesty, famed for her pose. Is
anything lost when she's seen through glass,
through pixels and optic nerves? What changes
when a picture is framed? Who is inside it, and
who is ashamed of their place there?

Today, I asked the robot where to find the
fountain. She showed me, in Immersive
View, which is new, which is where, from space,
or maybe from scratch, or from the
movement of our own eyes, she has pieced
together the Fiats and cobblestones.
She hasn't quite gotten the tops of trees right,
the leaves and their branching, so geometric
they should be easy. And she's gotten
the statue at the fountain's center all
wrong, rendered without detail, a lump
of stone with pixels spraying from where
his mouth should be. She's got this all wrong.
It wasn't like this, it's not like this at all.
This isn't how I remembered the world.
And in telling her this, I make her better.

Notice the veins of David, in his arms and in the imperfections of the marble, stains from centuries of pigeons. Notice the art students hurrying away, rolling their sketches done in neon colors. Notice the first male nude in one thousand years stands twisted, lopsided, like I do, unless seen from a certain angle. Notice the wealth in all of this too. The outfits. Posing as a display of wealth, the luxury of time stood still. I can see his ribs, but I'm thinking of your belly. Notice the moment stood on end: before the shot, the confidence of the victor before his victory, stilled in the museum built to house him.

And notice Angelo, who sits next to me on the terrace, smoking, and asks to play a song for me. Whistling, he says he writes poetry, and here too, he has a problem with the government, *says they do not care about the poor people and are a little bit fascist*, and then breaks into *Knock knock knocking on heavens door*, with Bob Marley sprayed onto his guitar, but only makes it through a few lines before losing the words, and then changes into something Italian.

VI. Portovenere

My host, Ettore, tries to find the word for
griddle. He has made for me testirolli, which is
pasta that they make only in this region, on the
sea between Tuscany (pointing at the rim of
lights across the bay) and Levante (pointing
north, past the train station). He spreads his
hands flat, speaks of a dark metal, heavy and
black, and I find his word for iron that tastes of
blood.

Comosedice my grandmother, too, *spooned lard
into a pan like this.*

He mimes a cover for the skillet, a little oven,
from the word for the winged women who are
angry all the time. He circles the size of the fire,
says it must be fed with small wood: *kindling,
twigs.*

I tell him outside, from my window, dai fenestre,
I heard the nose of the wild boar, audio nasone
con cinghaile. Comosedice *snuffling, oink*, with
my fingers rooting in front of my face.

I tell him the wine tastes like *muscadines*, not
moscato, but from grapes in Tennessee with
thicker skins, difficult pelts, forte leather.

He shakes his head and smiles, returns to the
kitchen, la cucina, whistling along to the grateful
dead.

Comosedice, last night I dreamt of a cobbler, in
his basement workshop, resoling crocs, and I
hear, not quite a ringing, but a pressure that
releases from the small muscles of my jaw.

VII. Venice

The Peggy Guggenheim Collection

After all that marble, here, at last, is some clay.
Amphoras with sketches of terracotta skintones,
chitons and hair curled from brushstrokes.
This is the breaking of form. This is the piling of
shapes, one on top of the other. How do you
think this was made? Can you see the strokes of
the brush? Can you feel the way his hands
moved? This is the squeaking of rubber on stone,
the whir of the hand drier and the bump of
shoulders into strangers, neither of us paying
attention to our bodies in this space.
This is the snapping of a shutter.

Yesterday I saw an *October*, a Tintoretto, I think,
on the ceiling of the courthouse. This one was an
old man reclining, in grayscale to look like
marble, half in a toga, sighing with the passage
of time. Today I saw another *October* without
meaning to, a Kaminsky, and this one was so
different, a moon-face floating over the top of a
house. Sharp colors and semicircles, and still a

patch of blue sky. What does it mean? What does it mean to be making meaning of this? What does an October feel like?

In the same gallery was a Chagall, *The Rain*, with a house unmistakably of logs. My first evidence of a log house in all of Europe, not stucco or blocks of stone. And yes, there was rain. In this place, I wear the regalia of my people, thick pants with a bib in the front and straps over the shoulders, meant for working, but the girls here have no word for *overalls*, say instead *you are so colorful, or I like your jumpsuit, your outfit, gesturing up and down.*

Construct a body from this, I dare you.
Construct a meaning from this.

What's happening? What's the tradition, the legacy? What's it saying? Construct a politics from this, a bias. Why does this matter? Of course it doesn't, nothing does. Watch it move, let it breathe. Line as an automatic movement, line as an expression of the body.

VIII. NAPOLI

"Is that Vesuvius there, eh?

"Maybe. Not that big if it is, is it?"

Over one shoulder, a man with long hair and
sunglasses picks his guitar, capitalizing on the
parapet, the city view with its railing, with its
lovers, the day after Valentine's, kissing in broad
daylight. Over the other shoulder, a man in a
vest with his shoes off reads from a book in what
sounds like Russian. I can't tell what either of
them are saying. Behind me, schoolchildren
trickle from the museum, pigeons bobble over
the cobbles, and motorbikes roar to life. The
smell of sunshine and diesel. And in front of me
is the city, each of its windows and shaded
streets, and off to one side the mountain famed
for erupting. I have been surrounded by the
children on a lunch break from the museum,
each of them with a sandwich wrapped in tinfoil
and a few with cans of Pepsi, one with a thermos
of soup. They don't seem too downtrodden to
me, each with a warm coat and good jeans and
Nikes that still have their whiteness. And here

the chaperones, all women, follow the alleged
Russian as he makes his way through the crowd
of their children. And even when I want to, I
can't stop writing.

They've scented the museum with orange peels
and the flowers that grow here year round. The
emperor dressed for his coronation in white
gloves that fit tight to his skin, and tiny white
shoes, never meant for walking. The mountains
are the same as they are in the paintings, some
of the buildings are still here, but the light is
different, the fashions changed, the view not the
same as it once was. In the paintings, the
volcano is a source of both light and shadow, but
now everyone avoids looking, keeps their heads
down on the metro, won't watch the man who
plays accordion. Here there are mosaics and
frescoes and scale models and statues bronzed
and marble and silver and glass. And in the
middle of it all, in a glass case on the floor, the
cast of the body of a woman, the impression she
left in the ash, lying facedown, covering her
mouth with her forearms, her skirts hiked above

her hips. In the same way, a mosquito bites the marble breast of Psyche, and I try sambuca, a carminative that settles the digestive tract, that the robot tells me alleviates cramps and convulsions, and when I ask the bartender if it's true he hands me another tiny cup of coffee and warns me of the sugar flash.

Does it burn going down? Watching the shadows move across tile, wondering how you clean spray paint from stone, how you would sculpt a mound of blankets, sheets of cardboard, to show a person underneath. Who tends the grapevines in the city of the dead? Who dusts the ashes from the plaster-cast remains? Who feeds the cats in the room full of pots, all of them broken. Can you imagine the men on the metro, naked save for a helmet, fingering a spear, stones, an apple?

Nobody told me how wonderful this was, each line. Each curl of movement. Has anybody ever seen this Venus, the same tilt to her head, the same hip-curves, the same attending angels, in shards of a different clay.

The smoke and the daisies, daffodils blooming in my front yard while I'm not there to see them. Every dandelion I check says I'm in love and I believe them. I know what the petals will say when I count them.

The diver is chiuse for lavori, and if lichen is yellow that means it's alive, eating away at the limestone, at these shells of shells, remains of the temple to the god of the sea, which has moved a mile away from here. But here, finally, cars in a yard, the smell of goat.

Salivating over every scrap of English, over words flowing from my tongue. To drawling at people who understand me, idioms and complicated tenses. The pleasure of language observed. I'm looking forward to y'all'd'a'been, to fixin' to. To air thickernall getout.

Many of these problems have been easily solved in Dixie, if none of the others.

And someday I'll write something about my last night in italy, when the Brazilian communist in the bunk bed above me convinced me to go

tailgating to the soccer game, which wasn't
tailgating since there were no trucks with gates
to tail. And she was disappointed because she's
used to the Brazilian tailgating, not to the people
who line up and then enter the stadium. And we
went with a Japanese TikToker who just came
from spending three months in NYC, where
every day he would go to Times Square and film.
Himself, walking around, I guess. One time, he
rode the subway for 24 hours straight, for fun,
and said he filmed the homeless people sleeping.
That he would wake them up and film them, and
that sometimes they would fight, and he would
watch and film that. And me and the communist
laughed uncomfortably, in the tones of people
who have seen poverty up close, not mediated
by a screen. Who have experienced
homelessness, and hunger, and the vulnerability
of a body. And this whole time I've been worried
about looking like a tourist, about appearing
uninformed, of traipsing around with my
luggage and gawking for too long. And the
danger is real. Last week, in Salerno, I took one
picture, *one*, of the Amalfi coast spread out

behind me, walked further along the beach and sat down to read. Alone, in a quiet place. An hour later, a man from Gambia showed me his Italian documents and said he saw me take the picture, how then he knew that I wasn't Italian. He asked me where my hotel was, if we could be friends, if he could have my number. I wish I knew how to say *go on somewhere*.

Arrivederci, every brush stroke and chisel mark. Gilt and color and cobbled stones. Every noodle and grain of flour, tomato and ripe citrus. Every pigeon and fancy dog, mattress and wafered pillow.

IX. Athens

I'm drinking a glass of amber wine, which is made from white grapes with their skins left on. Halfway through, a man walks in from the street and tries to sell the restaurant a bottle of barefoot pink moscato.

I'm in a church where now it makes sense. The alabaster windows, the paintings dulled with smoke, incense that still burns, that tickles my throat. Let my eyes adjust, picking out the scrollwork on the wooden altar. The twinkle of chandeliers, unlit save for refractions, reflections, and even now I feel so small. A woman goes around and kisses all the paintings, the little ones off to the sides, in a part of the church I've forgotten the name for. Is this the body this was built for? The gold dulled, worn, the angels looming, the face of Mary on the throne, invisible, when this whole time I've been staring straight into the faces of altarpieces in fluorescence, behind glass, and never did I feel this presence.

And here I am, wishing Michelangelo had never invented those windows, had let me keep this quiet place, out of the sun and noise of the world.

I'm sitting on the Areopagus, the hill next to the Acropolis where I've heard St. Paul first preached the gospel to the Athenians. Where, guess what, the teenagers are smoking weed. I came up the back way, through the olive groves, where I encountered my first pile of European shit. And I thought, that's a good place to shit, in this pit, dug by hand, in the corner where the sacred grove backs up to the cemetery wall. I who've lived rough too, and shat in what woods there were, away from what's left of the market, as private as is now possible.

My bunkmake tells me of a man she shared a hostel room with, from Liverpool, in Turkey to get a set of new teeth. He had a strong accent, accentuated around his mouthful of gauze, and would haunt the rooftop bar, stumbling back to his bunk in the early mornings. One night, she woke to find him gone, asked the desk workers if he'd finally healed. They said he had hit on some Muslim girls and gotten his teeth knocked out, again.

I'm at the Propylaia, the sacred gate entering the Acropolis. It's morning, they just opened. In front of me, a woman sits on the steps, worn smooth with the passage of millennia of sandals. A man is taking her picture. He says "look like you wanna be here! Say *mama mia!*"
Inside, the guard yelling at tourists throwing gang signs. Deleting pictures, posing like Hercules. Disrespectful, spiritual place, not a stadium. *I know better than you do, my lady. We are living in a dark age, think about it.* In a sweatshirt, with a whistle. *I tell you from the beginning, you are making me alarm everybody. This is a satanic symbol, do not try to tell me this is "I love you" I know better than anyone. This is the history of gangs in my country. I tell you this because I don't want to inform the police. They give you a fine. You understand, yes? A fine, a*

payment. You can take pictures, but why don't you take normal pictures, like a tourist, okay? Look at her, look at this lady, he points to a lady spinning, arms outstretched, grinning over her shoulder. *You see how silly she looks? That is okay, you take pictures like this one.*

What else are you supposed to do except take a picture? How else are you supposed to contain an experience, moderate an overwhelming feeling?

Who am I to give my take on this place that's been here for thousands of years? I who've just read my first street sign, *People of Piraeus*. I who've just figured out how to avoid eye contact with restaurant barkers, how to move with a herd. Turn a corner and there her house is, looming. Obscured, distant, but looming. And the cats, that every single person in the city says *pspsps* to, builds little sanctuaries for, and the evil eyes for sale on every street.

controlled burn

After sunset, we wind up to the overlook,
squinting against headlights, an owl backlit,
spooked up from roadkill. We watch the swath of
pink ebb from the sky, colors too bright from the
haze. Your dog pulls down the trail, still, whines
into the darkness. In every other car, a pair of
teenagers, vaping out their sunroofs.

We watch our forest in a burn we've been told is
controlled. The fire is across the lake, the body
of still water. If we duck under the dashboard
and time our glances up between highbeams, we
can see the rim of light cresting the ridgeline of
mountains whose names we both know, whose
spines we had promised to walk over together.

Neither of us can sleep for the brightness of the
sky, for the jake brakes and orange lights and the
thinking, the pawing of the dog at our feet.

What if this is the last time? What if this is all
there is, and the rest isn't stars but planes and
streetlights, and ashes cover the mirror of the
lake?

What if we're wrong? What if we're not enough?
What if the forest is so changed we can no
longer see the trail, lose eachother in the piles of
burnt logs?

Then, your voice like a rope thrown into a hole,
like the froth of water in motion.

As soon as you stop fighting so hard, the fires
burn out on their own.

This is the truth, this is the worry, this is the
hose for the blaze.
This is the pull of hair, the taste of breakfast.

This is the smell of smoke, lingering in the valley.
This is the haze of another sunrise.